D1716587

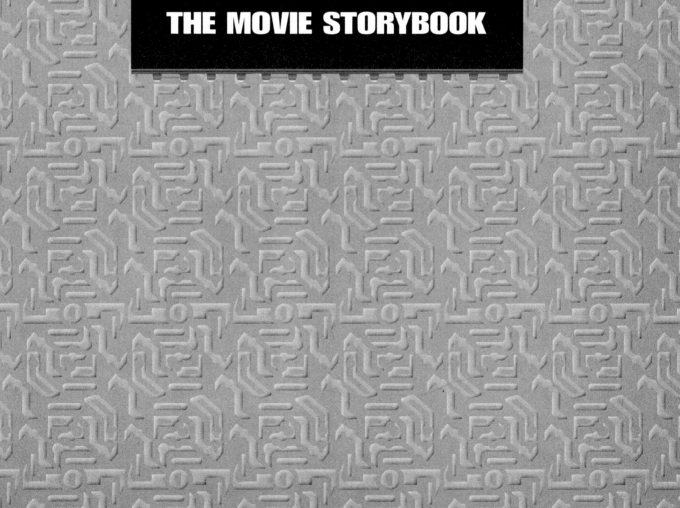

SMALL SOLDIERS

THE MOVIE STORYBOOK

SMALL SOLDIERS ™

THE MOVIE STORYBOOK

BY JENNIFER DUSSLING

BASED UPON THE SCREENPLAY
WRITTEN BY GAVIN SCOTT
AND ADAM RIFKIN AND
TED ELLIOTT & TERRY ROSSIO

DreamWorks ™

Irwin Wayfair and Larry Benson were sitting in the Globotech boardroom, nervously awaiting the arrival of their new boss, Gil Mars. Everyone else at Heartland Toys—make that Heartland Play Systems—had been fired, and they were next if Mr. Mars didn't like their presentations today. Talk about pressure.

The boardroom door opened, and in strode Gil Mars. He didn't waste any time. "What do you say we talk about the future?" he said, pointing to Irwin.

After nervously fumbling around trying to open his portfolio, Irwin spread a collection of drawings on the table. He looked fondly at his newest toy line—a bizarre bunch of

monsterlike action figures. "These are the Gorgonites," Irwin explained. "Now, this one's Archer." He pointed to his favorite, a gentle-looking creature with a crossbow slung across its back. "Their noble captain. They're lost in our world, and they want to get home to the Land of Gorgon." He pointed to another picture. "And this one's Troglokhan. He's the . . ."

"Stop! Stop!" Mars shouted. "I hate it! Next!"

Larry presented his idea—the Commando Elite, a line of superhuman army men. This time Gil Mars _was_ interested. "These toys should be the most advanced toys the consumer has ever seen. What I'm saying is that when kids play with these toys, they're so smart they play back," Mars said. His eyes fell on Irwin's Gorgonite sketches. "And what do soldiers need? Enemies! These guys!"

Irwin started to protest. This was all wrong! His Gorgonites were peaceful. They would rather hide than fight! And what Gil Mars was talking about—the talking, the fighting—cost major money. But already Larry was smiling confidently.

Irwin put his head down. He knew he shouldn't have gotten out of bed this morning!

Fourteen-year-old Alan Abernathy stood behind the counter of his dad's toy store. The Inner Child was a small, cozy shop filled with old-fashioned and educational games and toys—and empty of customers. His father was away on a business trip, and Alan was in charge for the day. Actually, Alan was surprised his dad was trusting him. After all, Alan had been kicked out of two schools back in Chicago. But he was determined to do a good job and make his father proud of him once again.

With that in mind, he had convinced Joe, the deliveryman from Globotech, to leave behind a set of Small Soldiers, the latest line of action figures from Heartland Play Systems. The Small Soldiers—the Gorgonites and the Commandos—were cool. They were exactly the kind of toys kids loved, and exactly the kind his father

hated. His dad's store carried stuff like board games and his special handmade wooden boats. In other words, bor–ing! With the Small Soldiers, maybe—Alan crossed his fingers—they'd even make some money for a change. Then his dad would <u>have</u> to admit Alan was responsible!

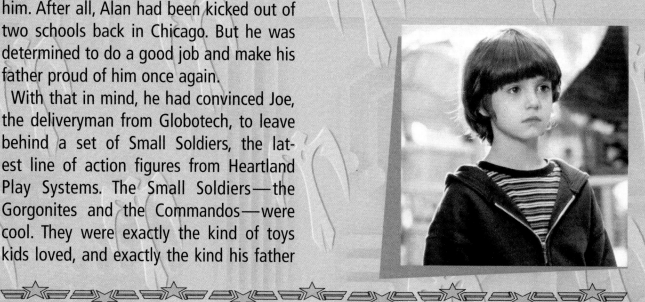

As Alan unpacked the box of Commandos, he looked up to see his neighbors Christy Fimple and her little brother, Tim. Alan immediately broke out into a nervous sweat. He found pretty, blonde Christy quite crushworthy. Tim took off to explore the store. Alan took a deep breath. Here was his chance to impress Christy. He'd better not blow it.

The two had just started to hit it off when Tim ran up to his sister, rubbing a red spot on his forehead. "I want the soldier," Tim said. "They were walking and fighting. They're so cool!"

When Alan told Christy the price of the toys, her eyes widened in shock. "There's no way Mom and Dad are going to buy you one of these," she told Tim.

"Yes they will!" Tim insisted. "They buy you your Gwendy dolls!"

Christy turned a deep shade of red.

"Massage Therapist Gwendy?" Tim added with a grin.

Christy gave her little brother a death stare. She had a reputation to uphold!

"Look," Alan said. "I'll hold it for you till tomorrow."

After Christy and Tim left, Alan locked the door behind them. It was time for him to head home. He ran a quick check of the store. Doors locked—check. Lights off—check. Cash register empty—check. He smiled. Everything was under control. He grabbed his backpack and made his way home.

In his room, Alan sat down in front of his computer and reached into his backpack. "What the—?" He jerked back as if he'd been bitten. Something was inside! Cautiously he peered in. It was just that dumb Gorgonite toy. "How did you get in there?" he asked, pulling Archer out.

"Greetings. I am Archer, emissary of the Gorgonites," the toy said mechanically. "What is your name?"

"I'm Alan, now shut up. I've got homework," Alan replied, turning to his computer.

"Greetings, Alan-Now-Shut-Up."

Alan whipped around in his seat. "What did you just say?"

The toy was silent.

"You just said my name," Alan accused him. But there was no response. It must have been his imagination. Shaking his head, Alan went back to his homework.

Late that night, after Alan fell asleep, Archer crept over to the computer mouse. <u>Click</u>. He pressed the button, scrolling through the Microsoft Encarta CD-ROM that Alan had been using.

"What are you?" Archer jumped back from the screen. Alan was awake, staring at Archer in wonder.

"Greetings. I am Archer, emissary of the Gorgonites," Archer said in a robotlike voice.

But Alan wasn't buying it. "I think you're smarter than you let on. Walk to the end of the desk."

Archer paused, then did as he was told. "Alan. Friend of Archer. Defender of all Gorgonites. You must help us."

Alan was puzzled. Archer tried again, but his voice chip was limited. He could not explain in the way he wanted. "There will be no mercy. The Gorgonites must be free," he pleaded.

"Maybe you're not as smart as I thought," Alan said. He looked at Archer, then stuffed the little monster into the desk drawer and closed it tight.

At The Inner Child, it wasn't the Gorgonites who were free. It was the Commando Elite. A pile of ruined boxes, their plastic windows punched to pieces, littered the floor, and six soldiers stood in a row. Major Chip Hazard. Brick Bazooka, artillery. Link Static, communications. Kip Killigan, spy. Butch Meathook, sniper. And Nick Nitro, demolitions.

Chip Hazard faced his men and told them their mission. "Search out the Gorgonites—and frag 'em all," he said in a cold, heartless voice.

★ ★ ★

Alan unlocked the door to The Inner Child and stared in shock. "I am in so much trouble," he moaned. The store looked like a war zone. In fact it <u>was</u> a war zone. Broken toys, boxes, game pieces, you name it, were piled two inches thick on the floor.

Archer jumped from Alan's backpack, where he had been hiding, and ran down the aisle. With a cry, he came upon the broken body of Troglokhan, one of the Gorgonites . . . one of his friends. Archer lowered his head sadly. "Beware," he said. "There will be no mercy."

Alan looked at Archer. Now he thought he understood what Archer had struggled to put into words the night before. "This is what you meant? Who did this?" He noticed the empty Commando boxes. "Oh, no way."

"The Commando Elite will destroy the Gorgonites," Archer said.

Shaking his head, Alan grabbed a dustpan and broom and started to clean up. It took him all day. When the last bags of trash were tossed in the dumpster, he started home.

Alan did not even notice that he was being watched, that a Small Soldier had hitched a ride on his bike, almost to the very edge of his driveway.

The Commandos had located the enemy stronghold.

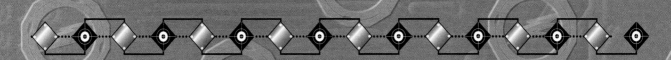

Inside the enemy stronghold, aka Alan's house, Alan slammed down the phone. After being transferred to countless extensions on the Globotech hotline, he had finally left an angry message on some geeky-sounding guy's voice mail.

He pulled on his headphones and flopped onto his bed. So only Archer heard the strange voice echoing down the hallway: "Beware. There will be no mercy."

Archer sneaked out of Alan's room. The voice was coming from a hall cabinet. Archer peeked inside hopefully, thinking he might find his comrades. But it wasn't a fellow Gorgonite. It was an ambush!

The Commandos quickly dragged Archer into the kitchen.

"Where are the rest of the Gorgonites?" demanded Chip Hazard.

Archer was confused for a moment. Then the question sank in. The rest of the Gorgonites? That must mean the other Gorgonites were alive! He smiled.

"Into the pit!" Chip Hazard ordered. Link Static flipped a switch on the wall, and from the kitchen sink came a low rumbling noise. It was the garbage disposal!

Archer's head came closer, closer, closer to the whirling blades when—

The kitchen was flooded with light. Alan stood there in shock. "Hey!" he managed to shout.

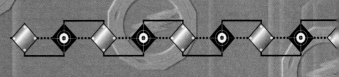

"Troopers, pull back!" Major Chip Hazard yelled. The Commandos scattered for cover. Brick Bazooka released the cord holding Archer. Alan lunged forward and grabbed the Gorgonite just before he fell into the disposal.

"Surrender, Gorgonite ally!" shouted Nick Nitro, as he attacked Alan with a small saw.

Alan grabbed the toy soldier. Again, Nick stabbed Alan. In self-defense, Alan thrust him feet first into the disposal. CR-R-UNCH!

"Uh-oh," Irwin said. He'd had a bad feeling ever since he received the angry message from that Abernathy kid. That bad feeling had just gotten a lot worse. He and Larry stared at the computer screen in disbelief. <u>Microprocessor: Globotech X-1000: Unit Cost $4,000.</u> Somehow, some way, super-high-tech computer chips meant for the Department of Defense had been implanted into every single Gorgonite and Commando Elite toy.

This was bad—very bad.

★ ★ ★

Alan brought Archer upstairs and set him down on the bathroom counter. Archer told Alan that his fellow Gorgonites were still alive. "My Gorgonite brothers are doing what Gorgonites do best," said Archer. "They are <u>hiding.</u>"

The next day, Alan and Archer went straight to The Inner Child and searched everywhere. But there were no Gorgonites to be found.

"All right," said Alan. "If I were a Gorgonite, where would I be? Okay, I'm hiding. I'm a loser. I've got zero self-esteem."

He thought hard for a moment. Suddenly a light bulb went on. With Archer right behind him, he ran to the alley behind the store and threw open the lid to the dumpster. A giant eyeball—with three legs—stared back at him.

"Ocula!" Archer said happily.

The bags in the dumpster shifted. Alan saw Punch-It and Scratch-It, Insaniac and Slamfist. And finally, Troglokhan. Or what used to be Troglokhan. The creature was patched together with pieces of broken toys and an old radio. He was quite a sight to see.

"We fixed him," Punch-It said.

"<u>Tried</u> to fix him," Slamfist added.

"Freaky," said Alan. "Like Frankenstein."

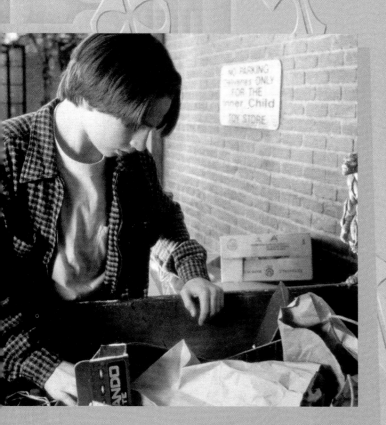

"Like Freakenstein," agreed Archer.

Alan found a cardboard box in the dumpster. "Okay," he said. "Everybody in."

Irwin and Larry walked into Globotech's clean room—the place where microchips were made. Everyone who went inside had to wear a white clean room suit so no dust or particles would be brought in, and Irwin and Larry were no exception. They looked like astronauts, ready for take-off.

Larry introduced himself to the technician who had supplied him with the X-1000 microchips. "There may be a problem," Larry said.

The technician grew angry. "The X-1000 is a masterpiece!" he said. "It can <u>learn</u>."

Irwin was shocked. "You're talking about <u>artificial</u> <u>intelligence</u>?" he asked.

"No," replied the technician. "<u>Actual</u> intelligence."

Irwin and Larry hurriedly left the room and removed the suits.

"I'm going to call Mr. Mars," said Irwin. "We have to recall the toys."

But Larry was not convinced this was necessary. They'd recall the toys sent to Alan's area code, and Alan's area code only.

"What about the toys he <u>has</u>?" asked Irwin.

Larry sighed. Like it or not, it was time for them to take a trip to Winslow Corners.

Plop! Plop!

The sound of sleeping pills dropping into two full glasses was drowned out by the noise from the TV. Christy's parents were so focused on the football game, they didn't notice anything else. Not the small shadows in one corner of the living room. Not the mini-missile launcher half hidden behind the couch. And definitely not the funny taste of their drinks. Soon their heads bobbed and both were sleeping soundly— and snoring loudly too.

Kip Killigan gave Butch Meathook a high five. Mission accomplished! The Commandos moved upstairs, looking for Christy. She wasn't home, but her brother was.

"Hey, cool!" Tim was walking past the open door to Christy's room when he spotted the soldiers. "I can't believe they got me the whole set!" He dropped to the floor to play.

Chip took one look at the kid. "Commandos, attack!" he yelled. The elite soldiers swarmed around Tim. Tim got into the game, kicking them off, slamming them to the floor, rolling them underfoot. He played rough.

"Okay. Now go ahead, capture me," Tim insisted. The Commandos looked at one another in surprise: Why was the enemy giving up so easily? But they were only too happy to obey. Kip and Butch wrapped fishing line around Tim's wrists and slapped duct tape on his mouth. Meanwhile Chip surveyed the area. His eye caught the shelves and shelves of dolls in Christy's room. Gwendy dolls.

But Chip wasn't admiring their long silky hair or their unnaturally small waists. He only had one thing on his mind. "Reinforcements," he said with a smile. "Bring Nick Nitro's body. Move!"

With the microprocessor chip from Nick's head, the Gwendy dolls were transformed from fashion plates to female warriors. By the time Christy returned home, Chip Hazard had a whole division of bald zombie dolls to carry out his orders.

Christy didn't stand a chance.

Ker-PLANG! Something shot through Alan's window.

"What was that?" Alan ran across the room. A missile, a barbecue-fork missile, was lodged in the wall. Pinned between its two points was Ocula.

Alan looked at the message wrapped around the fork. The note was simple—"Surrender"—and there was a videotape. Alan put it into his VCR.

The picture wavered, then came into focus. Alan's stomach lurched. It was Christy! She was a prisoner! And she would not be released until the Gorgonites surrendered.

Alan knew what had to be done. "If Major Chip Hazard wants a war, we'll give him a war!" he cried. He looked to the Gorgonites for support. But they were trembling with fear.

Archer shook his head sadly. "No, Alan, we will give up. It is what we were born to do."

Alan was furious. How could the Gorgonites give up so easily? "Stop doing what you're expected to do, just because that's how you're programmed!" he shouted. "Are you going to let yourselves get beat by a bunch of stupid toys?"

It turned out the Gorgonites wouldn't let themselves be beat by a bunch of stupid toys. With Alan's help, Archer rocketed into the Fimple house and let

Alan inside. The coast was clear. The Commandos were all outside the house gathered around a cardboard box they thought was filled with Gorgonites. Alan and Archer made their way to Christy's room.

There she was, bound and gagged. Alan winced. Those barbarians had even stuffed her pom-pom socks into her mouth! Alan ran over to her and cut the ropes.

"Behind you!" she yelled when he removed the gag.

Alan whirled around, just in time to see the Zom-Gwendies sneaking up on him. They knocked him to the ground. One of them charged at him, wielding a long, sharp sewing needle.

Crash! The Zom-Gwendies went flying across the room.

"You're all going to the Island of Misfit Toys!" Christy shouted. Alan stared in amazement as she swung a baton through the air, taking out doll after doll. Plastic heads, arms, high-heel feet, and other body parts scattered all over the room. Chip Hazard's doll division was history.

Christy helped Alan off the floor, then out of the blue, gave him a big kiss. "You rescued me," she said sweetly.

Alan swallowed hard. "Yes, I did," he managed to say.

Christy grabbed Alan's hand, Alan grabbed the backpack with Archer inside, and they raced downstairs. The Commandos had discovered that Alan and the Gorgonites had played a trick on them. There were no Gorgonites in the box—just a tape recorder! They were on red alert. Link Static drove around the carpet in a souped-up toaster tank that fired red-hot CDs.

Alan followed Christy through the open window. Once outside, they jumped on her motor scooter and sped away. But the soldiers were not far behind. A line of Commando attack vehicles with mounted weapons plowed through the garage door and raced after the scooter.

"Aaaah!" Alan screamed in pain. He looked down. Several razor-sharp corncob holders had pierced his leg.

Christy turned onto a bicycle path lined with tall trees. As they raced along, the trees started to explode and fall over. It was an ambush! Alan turned around—the Commando vehicles had joined together to form one mega-vehicle and it was closing in on them!

There was only one chance for escape—across a nearby stream.

"I dare you," said Alan.

Christy leaned over the handlebars, took a deep breath, and hit the gas. "Hang on," she warned.

The scooter flew through the air, over the stream, and bounced hard as it landed on the other side. They were across!

But Chip Hazard was right behind them. The mega-vehicle sped up, launched into the air—and smashed into the streambank. Ka-BOOM! There was a huge explosion.

Somehow Chip managed to remain in one piece. He floated downstream on a broken piece of mega-vehicle. The light on his belt was weak, flickering. His empty eyes stared at the sky.

All at once the light on Chip's belt glowed intensely. He sat up. A giant advertising balloon floated on the horizon. A Chip Hazard balloon.

It gave Chip strength. He struggled out of the water and up the streambank toward the balloon.

It floated above Toy World, announcing the arrival of the Small Soldiers.

"We have lost the battle," Chip said grimly. "We will not lose the war."

Chip soon had an even bigger and stronger army—made up of brand-new Commando Elite action figures from Toy World.

Alan was in trouble. When Christy's mom and dad finally woke up, their house was a wreck. They found Tim tied up in a closet, their appliances stripped for parts, and their daughter missing. Worst of all, they had missed the big game. The Fimples marched angrily to the Abernathy house, demanding an explanation.

Just then the Gorgonites appeared. So Alan told everyone the whole story. They all stared at him. Finally his father spoke. "I believe you," he said. Alan grinned in relief. This time for once, his dad believed him!

"That's it!" Christy's father cried in disgust. He stomped to the door and pulled it open. There stood Irwin Wayfair and Larry Benson.

With two employees from a major corporation like Globotech backing up Alan's story, Mr. Fimple finally had to admit that maybe the kid was telling the truth. That's when the lights went out throughout the house.

"Oh, no," Alan groaned. He moved to the window. Joe's delivery truck was parked outside. Joe had been taken hostage by Chip Hazard and was tied to the steering wheel. Squads and squads of identical Commando Elite soldiers were jumping out of the back of Joe's truck.

A mini-jeep came flying around the corner. Chip Hazard barked orders to his troops. The toys were back—and this time they meant business!

"There will be no surrender!" Chip boomed. "All Gorgonites will die!"

Even though Mr. Fimple was more than happy to sacrifice the Gorgonites, the attack began. Barbecue flamethrowers shot balls of fire at the house. A nail gun mounted on one of the attack vehicles stitched the windows with iron nails, making the glass collapse. Flaming tennis balls hurtled through the broken windows. Alan's mom grabbed a racquet and started hitting them back.

Irwin searched his brain for a way to stop the Commandos. Finally it came to him. "The only thing that might work," he said, "is an electromagnetic pulse. It would fry the chips."

Alan grabbed Irwin's shoulder. "The backyard!" he said excitedly. "There's a power pole back there. There are two huge transformers on it! Could we use those to make an electro-whatever?"

"If we could blow them up, it would work!" Irwin shouted.

To blow up the transformers, Alan would have to climb the power pole and connect them with a pipe wrench. And his father would have to distract the soldiers' attention.

Alan's dad flung open the door, rushed into the yard, and started whacking soldiers right and left with a broom. Father and son managed to make it to the side of the house. They huddled behind the sun porch. The nail-gun vehicle patrolled back and forth, and toy helicopters flew low passes. The power pole seemed impossibly far away.

Archer had witnessed the whole scene from Alan's kitchen. Despite his programming, despite the fact that he and his fellow Gorgonites were created to hide, Archer could no longer live in fear. Not when his friend was in trouble!

"Gorgonites! We must help Alan!" he cried. Out of cabinets, from all sorts of clever hiding spots, the Gorgonites came, one by one.

"No more hiding," Archer vowed, putting out his hand. All the Gorgonites covered it with their own—except for Freakenstein, still a little confused after his recent surgery, who added a foot, and Ocula, of course, who used his eye.

The door to the sun porch flew open, and with a crazy scream of laughter out stormed Insaniac. He slammed into a Commando, knocking him down. Right behind him came the other Gorgonites. Slamfist pounded the plastic out of a soldier, while Ocula wrapped his eye stalk so tightly around another that the soldier's head popped right off. Freakenstein grabbed control of the nail gun and sprayed the approaching Commando troops.

Alan stared at the brave Gorgonites in disbelief. Archer appeared beside him. "Alan, you may go now," he said.

"Archer, listen, when that thing explodes, you guys are gonna be fried, just like the Commandos." Alan choked on the words.

Archer pointed to the power pole. "Go."

Alan gave his friend one last look, then ran across the yard. When he reached the power pole, he tucked the pipe wrench into his waistband and started to climb up. At the top, he fastened a rubber hose around his waist and the pole, grabbed the wrench, and struggled to place it between the two transformers.

From across the yard Chip Hazard saw what Alan was doing. He jumped into a helicopter. The chopper zoomed in, rockets firing, and scored a direct hit to the pole. Alan lost his grip and fell—and dropped the pipe wrench. The hose stopped his fall with a jerk, his hands forced over his head. Chip came in for a second attack, yet just when Alan thought he was a goner, nails pierced the blades of the helicopter. Insaniac had saved him!

The helicopter plunged to the ground—but not before Chip could leap to the pole.

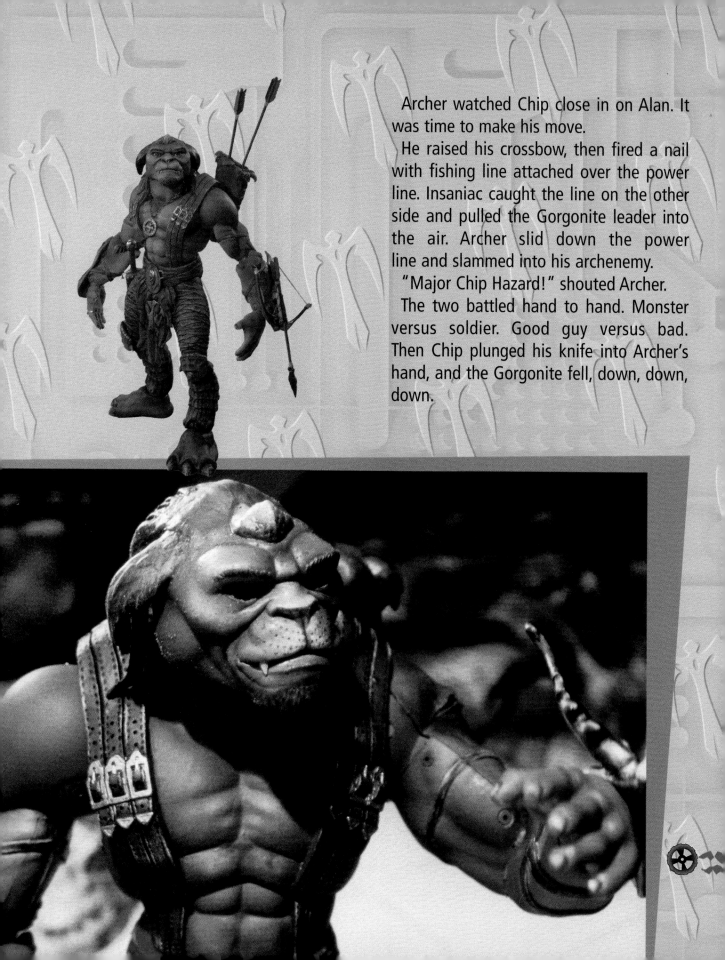

Archer watched Chip close in on Alan. It was time to make his move.

He raised his crossbow, then fired a nail with fishing line attached over the power line. Insaniac caught the line on the other side and pulled the Gorgonite leader into the air. Archer slid down the power line and slammed into his archenemy.

"Major Chip Hazard!" shouted Archer.

The two battled hand to hand. Monster versus soldier. Good guy versus bad. Then Chip plunged his knife into Archer's hand, and the Gorgonite fell, down, down, down.

Chip laughed. "Victory is ours!" he gloated.

"Shut up, you stupid toy!" Alan grabbed the soldier and jammed him hard between the two transformers. Chip shuddered as the electricity ran through him. His hard plastic began to melt, bubble, and run.

Alan dropped to the ground. And in a giant burst of white-hot light, the transformers blew!

All across Alan's yard, the Commandos jerked to a stop. Their bodies melted, their heads popped off, the lights on their belts went black. The soldiers were dead!

The war was over.

Still, Alan could not be entirely happy. Sure, he had saved his family and friends from the evil Commandos. He had regained his father's trust. And he had won a new girlfriend—Christy Fimple. But in defeating his enemies he had sacrificed his friends, six very good friends. Friends whom he could not stop thinking about. Even after Gil Mars showed up in his helicopter, and presented everyone with a big fat check to compensate for the damage, Alan's thoughts went back to Archer.

Alan was cleaning up the yard, throwing dead Commandos into a pile, when an odd sound caught his attention. <u>Ding-ding-ding.</u> It was coming from an overturned satellite dish. Alan gripped the edge of the dish and turned it over.

Underneath were the Gorgonites. They were twitching, stuck doing the same motions over and over.

Alan picked up his friend. "Archer? Are you okay?" he asked hopefully.

"Greetings. I am Archer, emissary of the Gorgonites," Archer said. "Greetings. I am Archer, emissary of the Gorgonites," he repeated, like a robot.

"Oh man, your chip got fried . . . just like all the Commandos." Alan shook his head sadly.

Archer's legs stopped twitching. He turned to Alan. "The Commandos are dead?"

Alan gave a glad cry. Archer was alive! He didn't get fried!

"Gorgonites! We won!" Archer shouted. The rest of the Gorgonites came to life.

"Archer, I'm glad you made it," Alan said.

"I'm glad <u>you</u> made it, Alan," replied Archer.

"I guess the dish must have shielded you," Alan said in wonder. "Pretty smart."

"We did what we do best," explained Archer. "We hid!"

On a bright sunny day, Archer climbed into a beautiful handmade ship from The Inner Child. The other Gorgonites were waiting on board.

"You're sure you want to do this?" Alan asked. He didn't really want his friends to leave.

"Yes, Alan," Archer said. "It is time for us to go."

Alan took a deep breath, nodded, and pushed the boat into the water.

"Good-bye, Alan," the Gorgonites called. Alan stood and watched until the boat drifted off slowly into the mist and was no longer in sight. But he wasn't sad anymore. His friends were on an important journey. They were headed for the place the Gorgonites called home.